Collected Poems
of a Painter

George Claessen

COLLECTED POEMS OF A PAINTER

Edited by Irina Johnstone
With an introduction by Alistair Hicks

THREE HIGHGATE

First published in the United Kingdom in 2023 by
Three Highgate Editions
3 Highgate High Street
LONDON
N6 5JR

www.threehighgate.com

Copyright © The Estate of George Claessen 2023
Introduction copyright © Alistair Hicks 2023
Biographical copyright © Esmeralda Claessen 2023

The rights of George Claessen to be identified as the author of this work has been asserted by his Estate in accordance with the Copyrights, Designs and Patents Act of 1988.

A CIP catalogue record for this book
is available from the British Library

ISBN 978-1-7395449-0-4

Cover design by Tony Frazer

*Distributed by Shearsman Books,
PO Box 4239, Swindon SN3 9FN, United Kingdom*

ACKNOWLEDGEMENTS

The poems collected in this volume were in most cases previously published as follows: *Poems of a Painter* (London: The Mitre Press, 1967), *Poems about Nothing* (Ilfracombe: Arthur Stockwell Ltd, 1981), *Collected Poems* (London: Avon Books, 1995). Four uncollected poems have been drawn from manuscripts found in the author's papers, and a further poem, 'Lanka' was published, as a prize-winning poem, in the *Ceylon Morning Leader*, 30 May 1926.

CONTENTS

Introduction	9
It might well be	15
Vale	16
Fearing that I had lost you	17
Orpheus	18
The Hermit	19
O Muse of Poetry!	20
Let me lie in thy shadow	21
Like in seascape	22
Planets	23
Toccata	24
'The Sleeping Gipsy'	25
Moses	26
Joy from love	27
Death and the Puppets	28
O Moon	29
Rocinante	30
How the dissonant cry	31
Lost Love	32
When our dust is sifted	33
Bird of Paradise	34
Adam and Eve	35
Seek not Love's hidden features	36
Lines Inspired by Beethoven's Opus 132	37
The Horseman	38
Should change by art contrived	39
The River	40
Were flesh and bones unknown	41
Song of Love	42

Theorem of Pythagoras	43
Pastorale	44
Blackbird	45
Messe des Morts	46
The Mountain	47
Sailors	48
Where your eyes fade	49
There exists a delineation	50
Robot	51
How in my pious egoism	52
2 Stanzas	53
Flute	54
The Day	55
Dead Man's Cove	57
Prism	58
Beauty to me is you	59
'Seeing Clocks'	60
I hear a mocking laugh	61
It might be a notion to regard	62
Musical Box	63
Realist	64
Word	65
Vision	66
Quantum	67
This moment, now and forever	68
Tryst	69
Romanza	70
Where	71
Circle	72
Escape	73
Invocation	74
Sanctus	75

Voices	76
Time	77
Your thoughts search for me	78
Trinity	79
In the changes of light	80
Passion	81
Chiaroscuro	82
Cartouche	83
Berceuse	84
Faith	85
The butterfly escapes the clown	86
To the Memory of Donald Sinclair	87
Lines on an Apple	88
Covenant	89
The Card Game	90
Coda	91
Mardi Gras	92
Departures	93
Inscription	94
Aujourd'hui, demain ou au temps	95
Agnus Dei	96
Mother of the Muses!	97
Lanka	98
Rhyme	100
Cosmic Prison	101
Supposition	102
BIOGRAPHICAL NOTES	104

A NOTE OF THANKS

A special thank you to Esmeralda Claessen, Wolf Sulham and Astrid Alben for all their invaluable help and guidance with this book.

GEORGE CLAESSEN
– POETRY IN PAINT AND WORDS

'Home at last – it must be heaven,' sighed Claessen as he saw Britain for the first time in 1949. He glimpsed the rooftops and spires of Gravesend from the ship that had brought him from Bombay. Since his days during the Second World War as a founding member of the '43 Group in his birthplace, Sri Lanka, he had travelled to Melbourne and then India for some three years as the British Empire crumbled. His painting and poetry are a headlong flight from the devastating destruction of the nasty cocktail of nationalism and colonialism. Claessen remained in Britain for the rest of his life. In his pictures and poems he created a sense of belonging.

Claessen's art is aspirational: those spires seen at the end of a long voyage stayed with him and supplied the inspiration for what John Berger described in *The New Statesman* as 'those nervous good drawings of George Claessen.' He was relieved to reach London. He recalled sitting on a bench in a Bombay park and thinking 'this is it – I am going to end my time here.' He arrived in a city that was not only undergoing rapid social and political changes, but was also the refuge of many artists from abroad. The School of London was emerging at this time fuelled by the restless energy of the likes of Lucian Freud, Frank Auerbach, R.B. Kitaj and Leon Kossoff. These men, in the circle of Francis Bacon, all primarily worked in opposition to the dominant avant-garde art form of the moment – abstraction. Claessen had nothing against figuration. Indeed, he continued to make drawings, including those of spires, and portraits of those around him throughout his whole life, but he found a regenerative spirit in abstraction. His paintings illustrate the healing qualities of abstraction as much as any of his more famous contemporaries.

'I did try to make another dimension,' said Claessen, 'another dimension which I thought had been overlooked and not known in a mathematical sense.' In some of his later abstracts there is a sense of combining geometry and the spirit he was looking for, but he was still wary of trying to pin things down. In poem after poem, and painting after painting he is asking us to break out of the cage of our mathematical minds.

The '43 Group has defined Claessen's position in the story of art, but one must remember that this movement came into being in volatile and unlikely circumstances, and its international importance is only beginning to be fully recognised. Although George Keyt, the best-known painter of the group, was not there on 29 August, 1943, when Lionel Wendt, held the first meeting in his house in Colombo, Claessen was. Claessen was also the first honorary treasurer of the group. The movement was not only a rebellion against the Ceylon Society of Artists, but a rare Modernist attempt at that time to use some of their own cultural origins as the building bricks for a new art. As the poet Pablo Neruda – who had spent time working in the Chilean embassy to Colombo – wrote, the group was creating a new culture *'torn between the death rattles of the Empire and a human appraisal of the untapped values of Ceylon.'* The '43 Group (the founding members of which included Ivan Peries, Harry Pieris, Geoffrey Beling, Aubrey Collette, Justin Deraniyagala, Richard Gabriel and L.T.P. Manjusri as well as Keyt, Wendt and Claessen) was far more than just a collection of painters. Poetry was at the centre of all their art and almost all of them were practitioners of more than one art, reflecting Wendt's own wide vision: Wendt was a pianist, photographer, filmmaker and critic.

The group was created in opposition to Imperialism, but the turbulent times in Sri Lanka did mean that the '43 Group were not only diverse practitioners but were also dispersed across the world. Ivan Peries and Claessen both spent more than half of their lives in England.

With its fluid movement between poetry and the other arts, the '43 Group set Claessen on his steadfast path, that he trod firmly even in the long more isolated years in London. He wrote most of his poems and made most of his paintings in North London, his home for the majority of his life. Back in Colombo he was a figurative painter. There were hints of the abstraction to come in *Church by the Sea,* 1944, and even *Nude,* 1944, but they were only hints. Even if the '43 Group were demarcating their difference from South Asian art, both contemporary and of the past, Claessen did not make the leap into abstraction till he was safely settled in London, where abstraction had become the currency of the avant-garde. Despite this, Claessen's abstraction, is a world entirely of its own. He made a home in his art.

Two world wars, the genocides of Mao, Stalin and Hitler, the demonstration of the horrors of nuclear destruction in Japan, were certainly enough to make intelligent people question the way 'man' was running the world. There was a thirst for a new way of thinking and seeing. In 1952 when John Berger wrote the foreword to an exhibition of the '43 Group in South Kensington, he had a belief that artists outside Europe and America had more chance of making a 'new democratic art' as they had 'largely escaped the cultural corrosion of urban capitalism.' Even though, ironically, Claessen ended up living in a rapidly changing capitalist centre, to make his response, he did come to express 'the immediacy between art and life' and a 'Way of Seeing' for which the *New Statesman* critic was yearning.

Again ironically, as abstraction can be seen as the most distanced response to the world, it is in Claessen's abstract works on paper and his most transcendental poetic writings that we find a distilled immediacy. Claessen's abstraction manages to be aspirational and nostalgic at the same time. The music in the words and the paintings contain the dreams of the spires and heavens above but also one is aware of the rich, complicated and troubled past. The artist admitted that the 1914 Colombo riots and fights between Sinhalese and Muslims had a distinct impact on him.

Claessen is very successful in making a new abstract home for himself. Despite the political background there is a great peace in most of the pictures. While there are echoes of the spiritualism of Kandinsky, there is no heavy reliance on colour theories (i.e. which colours trigger which emotions). The world he creates is much calmer than Kandinsky's. He has built it up more like Cézanne's contemplation of Mont Saint-Victoire. Remember Claessen is a wordsmith! He treats paint like he treats the words in his poems. He is shifting them around like a child with putty.

Rather like Rabindranath Tagore, Claessen sees few barriers between words, music and painting. Ironically, for a man who fiercely denounced crude nationalism, Tagore wrote the national anthems for both India and Bangladesh. Claessen too fled the effects of nationalism but found his land with no borders inside abstraction. One can almost hear the sound of a calm sea in some of Claessen's works. They are generally peaceful, but we know what storms brew in the oceans. At the moment the little waves could be the result of a little pebble. The artist made a better world. He knew of the horrors out there, but was prepared to share his new enchanted waters with us all.

Any text on George Claessen has the risk of limiting his work, so I leave you with his words:

> 'This knowledge completely vanished
> In a matter of a few moments,
> Utter Simplicity of truth
> Passed beyond my comprehension'

Alistair Hicks,
September 2023

It might well be,
When lovers kiss in the windless garden,
Midnight rushes into noon's arms.
When outstretched Adam thrust upwards from his earth-bed.
As Michelangelo depicted, gazing at heaven,
His torso rising slowly to rest on supporting elbow,
It might well be,
A logic was revealed in a geometric law,
As simple and as timeless.

VALE

In the twilight of the clock
Each to relinquish,
To say goodbye. O never
To behold again your face,
Nor mine, in the eyes mirrored.
Empty the bough of famine,
All the buds scattered:
Softly, to leave you,
O my banquet of the earth!

Fearing that I had lost you in the throng,
With panic you I searched in vain; your track
To scan I sought before the spoor was lost
In crowding moments, soon to disappear;
When suddenly, I found you close at hand,
Around the comers of your mouth a smile,
And in your eyes a question as to how
It was myself I lost, strayed from a womb,
Of deep umbilical perplexities,
Terrifying with its tides, yet like the moon
Serene, indulgent, endowed to bear
With sorrows of a creature yet unborn.
Feared I lose what I might fail to find
On verges of obscure futurity?

ORPHEUS

O lost Eurydice!
My lyre is silent without you.
If you ever return
From the drear underworld,
How I would fête you,
With all the pomp of music,
Close as a lover to life's image.
I, Orpheus, who am immortal,
But who dies and is reborn,
Interminably, with hope's swiftness,
Will linger and wait
In the vast, eternal corridors.

THE HERMIT

We found shards in the buried city, in
What perhaps had been a hermit's hideout,
Scratched on with symbols by a being strange,
Gone far beyond his own conditioning,
Sanity in doubt, striving to define
State of reality on lost terrain.
He asked of fountain-head of life a breath,
Not air we know that brings us to decay
But element bestowed, disclosed to him
By humble trust as infantine reward.
Each cross inscribed a vanity removed,
Each curve the truth expanding from itself,
Were mystic marks, on clay now tender grown
With age-encrusted ruins of his cell.

O Muse of Poetry!
Touch the strings of my heart,
Draw thy hands across me.
I have no message to offer,
No hope too make known
But thy music pressed together.
Tear me apart, if your art
In the contingency of creation
Too strong, demands it.
I am but a worthless instrument,
Meant to be played on till I break.

When I am finished,
Other strings may end
What I so pitifully began.

Let me lie in thy shadow, with foolish,
Vain thoughts, undetermined wants; suffer
My importuning voice for this short while,
Between my waking birth and longest sleep;
I play at abstractions, bowed in sorrow;
Much to know, grow old with, unseeingly,
Pyramids in history in loose, desert sand
And ruffled bones in archaic gravel-pits,
Where bloodless veins and empty heart must rest.
Abstractions are easy to mime; pride and fear
Particularly, but love eludes me,
Too shallow my breath and heart too hollow.
I prostrate must lie; shield with thy shadow
My pale, bloodless veins and hollow heart.

Like in seascape an errant wave
Out of nowhere appearing,
Visions of you suddenly arise.

In the ocean the wave is lost
Only to reappear; in me, likewise.
Your essence lives on and hides.

Come when you like and go
Back to the dividing ocean,
With me confiding your ghost,
To appear suddenly, like that wave.

PLANETS

From forked tongues of the sun come prophecies,
Doom portents, sonorous intimations
Of impermeable darkness ahead,
To planets shaken to the core in thrust
Through nothingness, as they, to light clinging,
Are eyes of the impenetrable deep,
On power-infested, transcendental seas.
In that so brooding everlastingness,
Of boundaries unconceived, to limits dead,
From trajectory never to return,
Must glowering suns and satellites explore
Windless immensity that holds no end;
No ports to call in blackness voyaging,
Or anchors weigh, nor quays to moor against.

TOCCATA

Spark of life,
Heart's ember,
Flame out in tongues of fire.
Create.
Destroy.
Recreate.
Smoulder.

'THE SLEEPING GIPSY'

It was the moon brought the lion
To the sleeping Bedouin, lost
In Henri Rousseau's heart; the lion,
Tail erect and eyes like fire-points,
Searching the soul of the sleeper.

Sleep dark gipsy beside your lute,
Somewhere runs the waters of life
To quench the thirst of your longing;
Brother to the lion, long sought friend,
Would ever dreams come true in sleep?

Tomorrow's sun would surround you
With molten sand, mercilessly,
And flame in your veins; but Rousseau
Willed a moon, then the lion found you
Asleep, and searched your anguished soul.

MOSES

God spake unto Moses in the ghost-light
On Mount Horeb made manifest in fire.
Moses, seized with highest exaltation,
Had trembled like a leaf to hear his name
Struck on the glowing anvils of the Word.
A wind of thunder blowing through his ears,
Had wound the future round him like a cloak,
Had burst a sunken well of stubborn power,
Had placed within his grasp a serpent-rod.
His one God of intellectual grandeur,
Who for long supine had lain, the crux
Of all his unshaped own creativeness,
Had loosed the chains of fear inside his breast,
Had changed his outline against the sparse hills.

Joy from love fly not away,
Yield not to unreal cares
So few ephemeral hours.
Stealthily and hardly missed,
With the rose's pallid glance,
With the sadness of the rain
Falling on a poet's grave,
Whilst the lovers vowed and kissed,
Joy from love had flown.

DEATH AND THE PUPPETS

Here now to snatch the syllable of life
From all the puppets of this roving stage,
Comes Death, the bailiff of the shriftless shires,
Sullen and poker-faced, unhinging doors;
Whether or not with pain or swift of aim
To whisk them off, their chattels left behind,
All things undone, all hopes mislaid or lost,
Their cries and slogans fading hoarse and thin;
Sometimes with plumed steeds in funeral pomp,
Or tumbled shroudless in the swallowing grave.
To boss the stage in bailiff's coat; not take
Aught but these stiffening moulds, that once with truth,
Their frenzied roles had played; neither to care
Just how from each life's syllable had flowed.

O MOON

O moon! partner of earth's secret ways,
Say how you keep reflected in your face
The knowledge of a guided plan.
As with the weasel, mole or bat,
Of your recurrent surge
All nature in a swoon is made aware,
Transforming and transposing
Trees into grey spectres and lovers into swans.

ROCINANTE

Droll steed that galloped through Cervantes' brain,
Now graze in peace. Oddest of mounts, that bore
A gaunt and luckless knight by flinty paths
To Calvary; his fat and faithful squire
Straddling a donkey hard behind. Hear still
What peals of laughter ring the spheres; for oft,
The rider's fire had singed your flanks; often,
His madness changed the shape of things or made
A muttering fervency above, that lit
Your cryptic blood; by then you cared not how
Crowds booed or brickbats flew; thus vowed to bring,
Tight in the saddle, come tides of war or love,
Your crazed and towering saint in armour clad,
Through human suffering to surcease of woe.

How the dissonant cry of the newborn,
Its nostrils pierced by the quick of life,
Presages the anguish of its anxious flesh.

What contact has the human morsel lost?
Bereft of knowledge that there does exist
A tenderness, that is the Deep itself.

LOST LOVE

The flares of Eden blinded my eyes
On those desolate hills outside,
Those lonely morgues of silence
Hopelessly mute. I lost you there,
Groping to find you, my love.
Only the wild sobbing of your body I heard,
Till gradually it softer grew,
Softer and softer like the whispering wind.

My immortality went with you,
My unity with the cosmos, my understanding,
My strength, my godhead of calm.
I will search the centuries to find you, my beloved,
Employing every form and every known mask.
Heaven will open when I find you.

When our dust is sifted, our secret love
Will not be remembered, and you and I,
Vanished without record, will inhabit
An abstraction that sought not an abode
To trace on sand a temporal pattern;
Rather, having known, elected to keep
A sweet communication, like a breeze
That comes and goes to commiserate climes,
Sultry and warping, where the tread-mill turns.
If in that realm that man may never know,
Nor how could any man from hope withhold,
Where that integral part of us would go,
Then, then to claim that you for me I deem
My only heritage, my wages owed.

BIRD OF PARADISE

Somewhere in the moist, dark forest,
A bird of paradise, with tail
Whirring like a child's toy, there flies,
Living out its coma; its gaze
Fixed on the dream-ridden branches,
Its own intentions forgotten.

Like the presence of a comet,
Its whiteness flashes through the leaves,
Perfect, weighted to a feather,
Set in constant mysticism
In creation's deep pool, its flight
Flawless with instinctual aim.

Spinning tail and dazzling plumage,
Ambushed whilst on some errand bent,
Robbed of memory and detained
In forest depths of darkest green,
When cognizance could reawake,
Whither the true route would summon?

ADAM AND EVE

Coiled like a symbol she sleeps,
Limbs languorous and heavy,
In the drowsy dawn of creation,
Unaging, soft as a newblown rose.
Adam sleeps beside her, embalmed.
The earth has left them behind
On the fields of infinity.

Seek not Love's hidden features to disclose,
Or forever let the mind be haunted;
For Love is all unfurling, like a bud
Transfiguring to the status of a flower,
The first and greatest concept of the Word.
This magical beholding to our eyes
Is rarely offered in a mortal life,
When pride is carrying banners, or the mind,
Beset by gain, is shrinking from the truth;
But should it happen on some living day,
That you or I may come to such a sight
Of mystery, unworthy though we be,
Its primal spell that set the sun on fire,
Would drive us hungry for the face of Love.

LINES INSPIRED BY BEETHOVEN'S OPUS 132
(For J.S.)

Out of chaos a deep voice risen,
Herald of newborn hope soars upward,
Shouldering through broken-hearted debris.
A way to live, to praise describing;
Accept as now asserted, confessed.

Truth to what end? If unrequited
My craving Thy breath to breathe,
The primal, undreamed of union,
That towards Thee I might draw nearer,
With unutterable calmness, questing no more.

THE HORSEMAN

O untamed horseman! so be your coming;
I am ready, waiting with eagle sight,
Nothing of your approach to miss. No less,
Seized with the tremor of a rhythm wild
Of weird music coming from afar,
Indrawn and fateful, growing loud, until,
With pounding heart, I list, beyond the din,
The icy flute-calls in an arabesque
Of sound; whilst, in a gust the cold wind tells
You are abroad. I see you plainly now,
On pale steed mounted, riding saddle-free;
Borne on a rushing storm of hoofs, your cry,
Last that my ears will ever hear, rings out
For me, who else, in loud and clear halloo.

Should change by art contrived,
Replace with paltry words
Your tender, reckless sighs;
Should wells of kindness dry,
Or warmth be unretrieved,
Or nights to vapour fade
Like ritual incense,
Or unsurrendered be
To love your darkling gaze;
In now brief happiness
Of mellifluous hours,
Be enshrined forever
In succinct memory,
Aching bosom laid bare.

THE RIVER

Wide river, turbid and imperious,
Aroused to immense measure in your spate,
Sweep on unheedingly; your banks long burst,
The signposts gone and ordered acres drowned.
Flow quivering with flotsam to seek the arms
Of annihilating ocean; your griefs grown
Heavy for a season's rating. Be cleansed,
Your stricken bosom calm, return with love
To old haunts under the trees, a mirror
For clouds and birds; hardly to remember
The nightmare-days of floating sheep and men,
In ancient deaths from when the earth began:
Impartial, in a nature's law sublime,
Each stark awakening to resolve with time.

Were flesh and bones unknown,
The earth unmade,
If the deep was
Before the firmament,
Uncluttered, we would fall
Where we belong.

SONG OF LOVE

If I call into the void,
Would you hear me?
O lodestone to my mind.
If I cut an opening
Through infinity's veil,
Would the tryst be?
Failing, I would myself tumble
Through that square aperture;
Commence an endless fall
Towards your open arms.

THEOREM OF PYTHAGORAS

What metaphysical truth did Pythagoras assail?
Thinking far into the Grecian night,
Till over his head the dawn in Melos broke,
Bringing, in blessed sleep, forgetfulness.
Left with a bare theorem,
Still but a shadow only
Of what had scorched his brain
And rocked in awe his heart,
At such proximity to the Trinity.
Did he on his shoulder feel the hand of God?

PASTORALE

Lo! there stood a figure in the sky,
A great upright body of superb mien,
With big limbs musically at rest
That broke suddenly into a dance,
Of mighty gestures, perfect and voluptuous,
Posturing the quintessence of joy.

What shepherd loosened from his flock
Was dancing? while his own gigantic sheep
Were somewhere browsing. What unheard pipes
Were stabbing through his heart?

The giant form made aureate by the light
Exuded a glow of power,
The air was hot with latent fires
From nowhere slid the darkest cloud,
And with a thunderous shout, the figure fled

BLACKBIRD

All day long the blackbird
Never flags; each outburst
Pure, unfeigned: to listener,
Full of high expectancy
Of sound, the notes always
Redeemed though, are yet
As never before heard.

No simple task to tie
Its rapture down; logic
So inconclusive, set
In scale to prove a state
Of different being,
Cast as if on purpose,
Oddly, without a frame.

From sonant blackbird's throat
Stretched in the mounting theme,
An urge evoked to probe
Its singlemindedness,
And of the stranded bars
Of music, how they came.

MESSE DES MORTS

Creator of all things known or imagined,
Take unto Thee from this mortal body
That which Thou gavest – life and understanding;
That which is corruptible being consigned
To elements in the chemistry of change.
In thy abiding tolerance grant us
Remission of sins; from ignorance cleanse us.
May thy glory shine in our perception,
That the babel of our essential histories
May assume the purpose of thy creation.

THE MOUNTAIN

When this mountain broke
Its chains of unbeing,
The earth ran screaming everywhere
A cry too wild to hear.

It was a day of miracles;
Traumatic, sudden
Ecstasies of light,
The searing pangs
Of giant in prolapse,
The deep core eased
Of unknown, untold pain.

SAILORS

When the ocean in pain shrieks to the deck
From immense darkness of nights without faith,
Without stars or memory of light retained,
Even the sailor, inured to its ways,
Looks everywhere for solace as his heart
Drains of its blood; then in nameless fear pulls
Close about him the fleece of his lost loves;
As did Jason and his legendary crew
Grouped in tense sorrow on the distraught sea,
Till day returned customary rhythm
To their toils and boasts; whilst their own fears,
Assuaged in chores, dreaded the darkness
Of those nights when complete absence of light
Woke them to horror of a total loss.

Where your eyes fade
Is sheer cliff, falling
To immeasurable ravine.

When your voice, muted
To an echo, floats
In the abyss and fails;

When I can no more
See nor hear you, then
I am vanquished
Already, in mirage.

There exists a delineation of the mother and child,
Viewed from the sockets of an eyeless sight,
Drawn in an all-envisaging line
On sackcloth, in a dream hallucination;
With edges loosely flapping in the wind,
On barren wall, part of a structure
Built on summit, perilous and forbidding,
Full of pointed rocks.
How should be known the reason,
Pitched in this arid place,
For exposition of the Christ-child,
Where tigers must roam and serpents
Glide from rocky fissures over the sand,
Or the moon, rising in full, makes
Tremendous shadows and shapes.

ROBOT

In a waking dream I saw
An iron man; observed
His outstretched, steel fingers,
Metal palms advancing,
Barely pressing, snatching
What I had lived – moments
Packed in wooden boxes.

No strategy, no gun,
Unperturbed and final,
In lateral action,
His steel hands
Were deft and authoritative.

How in my pious egoism
Can I comfort thee?
From this nailed tree
All my deception recoils.

But if in me only
Nothingness I do wed,
My Jesus, afford me some grace
Thee to conjure.

2 STANZAS

On some bright morning,
When the sun is shining,
I shall sparkle around you,
Momentarily placing
A gold tiara on your head.

You would not know
Of such happening.
You would say –
'The sun is beautiful
The sun is so grand!'

FLUTE

Flute, stretch and coil,
Swim in a river
Of dark, shining facets;
Turn and gambol,
Utter your piercing shriek,
To fly like a ribbon
From shoulder to shoulder
Of terrible hills;
Silver, unanswered flute,
Frightened by lambs.

THE DAY

Why on that day? I ask myself,
Revelation experienced
At such an unexpected hour;
The sun blazing, high up in sky,
The noon heavy with life, oozing.
Yet it was then that I beheld
The microcosm, that I now,
On reflection, concede to be
My own soul, for want of meaning.

Haunting microcosm! that
Appeared not bigger than the span
Between mine eyes; yet in detail
Complete, precise in structural form;
Not foetus, but a man still-born.
I beheld without emotion,
Objectively, its naked limbs
Focused in light; now I recall
Clearly, review and analyse.

I could not then identify
This miniature as my soul;
Nor am I bound to recognize
It now. By what dubious mark?
Perhaps it was Adam, not me?
Squeezed out from clay, as though its frame,
Burnt to sepia in some kiln,
Deep stained red-brown by furnace heat,
Scooped up and left to cool as best,
Floated in locked trance before me.

Simultaneous to the scene –
There was this manifestation,
A silent swirl of power had come
At lightning speed; there sat revealed,
As on an unseen throne of air,
The God of life, his arm upraised.
I noted in his limbs a flush
Of swarthiness; his quiet face,
Viewed by me only in profile,
 I recall especially how
His nose and forehead were in line
Almost, as in certain Greek heads.

In that surreal flash of sight,
Held in a strange lucidity,
I watched the microcosm shudder,
Respond to life and I at once
Absorbed the logic of the act,
And still emotionless but rapt,
Its mathematics understood.

This knowledge completely vanished
In matter of a few moments.
Utter simplicity of truth
Passed beyond my comprehension.

DEAD MAN'S COVE

I know not on what bizarre shore
Of ocean I found myself, or why,
Inscribed indelibly, my imagination
Can revive in particular that scene,
Decked in strange, unearthly light;
Can recall menacing forms
That watched me from the entrance
Of a shack; hidden by dark,
Clustering trees, in sight of waves.

Figures of men who once lived,
Crowded weightless shapes at door,
To frown on my retreat, my trek
Over dry, yellow sand
To the boat that took me away;

With relief to be gone; to forget,
If well I could, that coast
Of miraculous light and strangeness;
Uncharted in accepted topography,
Its whereabouts unknown to navigation.

PRISM

Every hue and nuance
From the prism comes. Red
As of cascading blood,
Truth's dour, acid yellow
And love's unblanching blue,
 More violent than death,
Splintered to reassert
The triple primaries;
Translating from aura
To sounds and touching forms
In dark vaults that carry
Haunted imagery.

In a visible world
Within the certain sphere
Of its chromatic light,
In mirrors, reflecting
Tints that follow drama
From entry to exit,
To register, deployed
In terms objectively.
Nor that a fractious ray
Gone wild, could ever break
Its sheaf of hues, nor yet
Invent one more primary.

Beauty to me is you,
You are truth and alive.
Without rhyme or reason
I must love you,
That a kingdom shall continue.

However, I shall betray you,
Exchange love for words I coin.
Beforehand, all this
Was known to you.

I hold a fresh clue –
Yes, I imagine I possess
The truth. Let me illumine
My labyrinth with candles,
Whilst you recede
Into my dark mirror.

'SEEING CLOCKS'

Whoever you are
Who sits outside this chalet
In a shiny, white dress,
With supernaturally glistering eyes;
Blind as a doll is – yet seeing,
Only because of two supposed clock-faces,
That are merely holes in the wall
Under each of the twin gables,
Whilst their pendulums swing
Rhythmically, gaily, almost perkily,
Like metronomes.

I watch,
As you sit there, looking
Not at me but imaginary things.
What clocks are these that confer sight?
In what township must this chalet be?
You answer in thought. I know your name.

I hear a mocking laugh
Around me and feel
An eagerness rise up
In my empty hands.

As in a moment
In fractured light,
To sense a deception
Pale and derisive.

In accepted disbelief,
Facing an unknown void,
I turn to follow you
In avenues of illusion.

It might be a notion to regard
The abstraction of perfection
As the abstraction of nothingness;
Perhaps, not as foolish as outwardly seeming,
It might point to a definition of truth.

MUSICAL BOX

Play, play on,
On, on,
Always beginning,
You I know as I know you,
Play on, on,
I go with you,
Live on, on,
You are me,
Continuously, you are me,
Are each to other,
One, one only, one.

REALIST

Only tripartite God,
Such be as truth,
So exactly is,
Without antithesis,
Both male and female,
Could bind reality
Into substance;
Create from it
Sentient form
Of man or sparrow,
Leaving unconscious imprint
In its memory.

WORD

Words and their meanings are all withdrawn. Like
A bare hive the body lies with open eyes,
Retracted in a metaphor of glass.

VISION

A kingdom grew
With simple precision
Out of an earthen pot
In the mind of Stephen Smith age 7.
A plant of unusual floral diagram
With pink leaves: but was I not
Looking at a world in mass
From impregnable first principles,
Inside a singular periphery,
That no other could fix but he.

QUANTUM

It would take faith
To walk the tight-rope
Of infinity – the base-line
Of imagination set in triad,
In linear abstraction;
Its three angles tautening
In unimaginably dimensionless concept.

This moment, now and forever,
You have made me from dust,
Given me life – how strange.

My creaking bones and fitted joints
Co-ordinate and move,
Created for the first time.
You are trying me out – your machine.

My senses understand you;
My sustenance your blood and body;
I breathe in you.

For me being or unbeing is
Equal from now on.
In mathematical expression
I am everlasting – eternal.

TRYST

'Where should I find you?'
Somewhere in imagination
Is a crater starkly illumined –
A startled circle –
An area without reverberation,
Where thought articulates
Without tongue or a language,
Where time is an allegory.
Here confront me, my beloved,
With uncritical certainty.

ROMANZA

Owls hoot in trees
By pathways in forests
In the Mona Lisa's eyes –
Leading nowhere – only
To rhythms in poems
Unspoilt by meanings.

Against the owls' continuum,
The young hunter's horn blares
Clearly and distantly, as
He rides over the skeleton-leaves.

WHERE

In where,
In preternatural light,
Stillness is body –
Sight absorbs,
Pyramidically,
Three aspects of Time –
Thought speaks.

On hissing seas
Of silence,
To arrive, illogically.
With woodcutter's axe –
Amidst unexpected trees,
To stand transfixed.

CIRCLE

An inscribed circle is dross
To what lies outside it.

Unthinkable with infinite radii
Only the eucharist would result.

ESCAPE

Colour, shape and sound,
Transposing to one symbol,
Pass unscathed through
The tower of Babel
To abstraction.

INVOCATION

Setting and location have disappeared
To the point of being inconsequential.
You freely range, reappear
In visionary transmutation.
You come to the cry
Of a microcosmic voice
On the forlorn hills of charity.

Come now! I implore my
Movement's abstraction
Wildly to dance,
Standing on the slopes
Of such invisible hill,
Crying into the hollow
Of eternal causation.

SANCTUS

Words have existence
Shape and symbolism
Beyond ordinary function;
Each possessing consciousness
Individual and separate.

Seeming bodylessly to live;
Invisibly, voicelessly
To act and interact
In measureless equations;
Inviolable, protected.

VOICES

I shape my words to silence
In the conch of your ear.
Nothing the ocean, the sky,
In a listening shell;
From its spirals, the wind
Always tells of nothing.

In the fission of knowing,
When mirrors tilt inwards,
No more intercept, dissolve
Into a visionary dimension,
Voices of words would reiterate
My silence, in your ear.

TIME

In summation of moments,
My being with yours
Would fuse in oneness.

Would be replaced,
As with Adam and Eve,
By one word-symbol.

Your thoughts search for me
Over trackless wastes. Wherever
I am, you find me.
I do not err by conjecture –
I am aware of your power.
You are as I am; for I, too,
Search for you, in hopeless fashion,
To the gates of prophecy.

TRINITY

A pellucid kingdom of
Immortality – a principality
Of imagination made real,
Of thought quickened to life,
Would be revealed
If the door of the Trinity should open.
Of the absolute – tangible and child-like,
Only the word of seeing could define,
The touch of surrender make sudden discovery.

In the changes of light
That are so fickle and evanescent,
I will hide the distillation of moments,
So time could not pluck them from me.

Hence, they will be mine yet not so,
For the light would not return them
Specifically, but assimilate only,
Reappearing in misty, chromatic affirmations.

PASSION

His hands had nth power,
Were tenderer than Mary's;
His eyes, lost in imagery,
Already glazing.

As what was said, remained
As parables to accompanying miracles,
Incredulously accepted;
The crystal-clear innocence –
A metaphysical geometry
Incarnate in his being,
Remained ungrasped –
The cohesion of infinite future with infinite past.
In the timeless Word.

CHIAROSCURO

When I consider that light
Would have a non-existence,
Independent of darkness –
Darkness an unbeing of its own,
Your image, existent or not,
I worship, O antecedent God.

CARTOUCHE
for Michelle

Here is the stone pyramid and burial chamber,
Hard as night-frost,
That the desert fox cannot ravage
With its teeth and sandstorms cannot scathe.
Your lips are as ripe figs:
Your body is an obelisk of agate.
The heron, symbol of eternity, has lifted up its legs
       from the marshes and begun its flight.

BERCEUSE

In the hollow of the indigo night,
my love, she comes to me,
and her voice is as the song-bird
in the haunted tree in the field.

FAITH

When arts contrived
disown by stealth
safety in your embrace,
past happiness
of succinct memory
is impawned.

The butterfly escapes the clown
Of monstrous boots and large behind;
Nor ever will the net ensnare
The butterfly; nor clown
Renounce his chalky grin.
Perhaps, in deep, subliminal dreams,
A toppling cone in pink and white
Pursues in vain a minute cross;
To ease gently by recondite shapes
The sad, impermanent hopes of men;
Till clown-like, with stretched lips,
They lie in chalky, grinning sleep.

TO THE MEMORY OF DONALD SINCLAIR

He was to me by fate's accordance friend,
Held near in my affection; now is dead.
Continuance removed from comradeship,
That his compassion rendered firm and true.
What tribute pay in distant words to mark
His passing, when the struggling, mystic fire
In his mind smouldering now has flame? Ended
His search, his life to origin returned
In nature's offering duly made. For me,
Still left to ponder my mishap; recount
Comfort in one whose selfless vision brought
Rest and refreshment shorn of vanity;
Like to his quiet entry in the world,
Or his departure, made with noiseless tread.

LINES ON AN APPLE

Round, juicy, sap-heavy,
Future undecipherable, acknowledged
By the maggot-worm steering
To mingle purpose with purpose.

The bough that suckled you
Will disinherit; the tongue
of the lightning will unlock;

But, as from the beginning,
Indelibly incised, like
Your guest the maggot-worm,
In an invisible inventory.

COVENANT

This moment, now and forever,
You have made me from dust,
Given me life – how strange.

My creaking bones and fitted joints
Co-ordinate and move,
Created for the first time.
You are trying me out – your machine.
My sustenance your blood and body;
I breathe in you.

For me being or unbeing is
Equal from now on.
In mathematical expression
I am everlasting – eternal.

THE CARD GAME

He seats himself fatigued
Upon a stone, the ancient man:
Empties his pockets:
A crumpled pack of cards
Lurks somewhere in the folds:
Recalls past sixes and sevens,
Knaves of hearts and clubs,
She, his queen of hearts,
He, her king of same.
Yet none could block
The ace of spades. One must concede
The game was flawed, cards marked:
Gave her no chance, his ailing queen,
To last the rubber out.
He gathers up the cards wildly
And stuffs his pockets full.
Light is fading in the park.

CODA

The atmosphere had a viridian light,
Approaching noon, the day we stood
In front of Highgate church, looking up
At the façade with its cross.

It was November and the blood-red sun
Was balanced unforgettably in the sky,
 Like a melting-pot of all desire.
The pavement was full of passers-by;
Somewhere in the churchyard was the tomb of Karl Marx.

In these engraved moments of sun and cross
Is where I enshrine you.

MARDI GRAS

Above the white minaret flies
the bird of night. Droplets of water
are falling in the marble fountain.
Unmask, unmask, sinuous lady. An apple
rolls down the many steps.
A harlequin treads the circling ramp
of the amphitheatre,
and mute air fills the dawn's spaces.

DEPARTURES

The music-maker would say, the poet would say,
The artist would say and the dancer,
'Transport us first or Truth will forsake us'
'Pardon – to where?'
'Before Creation took place – point of reference –
anything you like', they say – 'set your clock there
and it will not go'
'Sorry – hold on!
But there's no such place,
Search how we may the timetable pages.'

INSCRIPTION
>   (À Alain Fournier)

Aides-moi à les retrouver – ces sentiers perdus,
Ange morne des arbres. Géant de la forêt,
Ou rôdent les gros clowns, gardiens des secrets de la vie,
Qui sautent partout parmi les papillons des idées
Et de qui nulle intention la plus intime ne pourrait échapper.

Ange silencieux! les empreintes sortent et reculent
Au delà de la logique enracinée: vous
Et les clowns, gardiens primordiaux, les connaissent bien –
Ces voies par lesquelles les saisons et les jours ensoleillés se
      sont envolés.

Aujourd'hui, demain ou au temps plus futur,
Je dois faire une promenade
Pour découvrir qui je suis –
Les entrailles de ma mère n'est pas assez.
Je dois casser mon prisme de couleurs,
Le rouge, le bleu et le jaune,
Trouver la sortie et faire un pas.
Je crois que ce pas m'emporterait
Dans un endroit sans supercherie,
Et la sortie s'ouvrirait
Comme les côtes du triangle qui tombent.

AGNUS DEI

Ma belle rose,
Fleur de mon cœur,
La Nature t'aime.

Les hommes savants
Sont partis
A califouchon
Sur leurs animaux.

Laissez-moi m'agenouiller
Près de vous,
À ne rien dire
Et à ne penser à rien.
Je t'ai vu aussi
Hier, dans ta beauté.

Mother of the Muses!
We come in costume
To mark the centuries with needle
And thread. Who would know
Our verses crumble like calcium in bones.

All we longed to say was said already
By the famous in a memorable way
Help us mother with the ruffs on the collar.

LANKA

Tall elephants with gilded cloths
With mahouts pricking at the ear,
And I shall tread on silver cloths
And dream of everything I hear,
The clash of swords and beat of drums
And kiss his feet if Rama comes,
Blazon the trumpets – he is near

Sakuntala shall sing to me
And speak the language of her eyes,
That be I either proud or cold
Shall tearless move me into sighs,
Till I could stake to kiss her lips
The scorn of slaves the slash of whips,
For great is love that never dies.

By Royal order I'll declare
To rear a palace like a peak,
Where resting I could gaze about
From one week to the coming week.
Four columns shall as landmarks stand,
And sun their lions golden grand,
Beyond these let the oceans reek.

Gold dagobas shall Kandy have
With temples full of costly lore,
Vast granaries to hold the seed
To touch the ceiling from the floor
Large tanks to still, of waters good.
And bridges made of satinwood
For men to pass and kings to go.

So would I regulate the land,
Till Lanka would resound once more
With Art and Learning hand in hand
And Beauty shall invade the shore,
To tone the mind and clear the eye,
A benediction from on high
My land to bless and fields to grow.

RHYME

Daphne is a tree
Garden 3′ x 4′.
I cannot know
If the Daphne knows
I love it so
Much. My love
Is pure. A storm
May blow, a flood
May be, a mountain
Fall on top of me
and my tree.

COSMIC PRISON

How sure? But yet escape there is
from tangled flesh;
take Excalibur from misgiving.

Warders in the firmament, uncountable
Encompass me; yet thought
Could bind, encircle them
To the last galaxy.
Slowly now! to float this glittering catch
Away – the Earth with it.

Then, my Lawgiver, my Triangle,
I'll be free to know You:
Unsay my searching for.

SUPPOSITION

So it must be, as living
Begs a question in its wake,
Timeless infinity the answer,
with subjective love, points
All creation to the grave.

BIOGRAPHICAL NOTES

ALISTAIR HICKS is a writer and an art curator. He recently curated Paula Rego shows at the Kestner Gesellschaft in Hanover, and the Pera Museum in Istanbul. Previously, he was a Senior Curator at Deutsche Bank. Alistair is the author of *The Global Art Compass: New Directions in 21st Century Art* (2014), *Urban Mirrors – Reflections from the Artists of Istanbul* (2022), *Art Works: British and German Contemporary Art, 1960–2000* (2001), *New British Art in the Saatchi Gallery* (1989), and *The School of London: The Resurgence of Contemporary Painting* (1989). He has also written as an art critic and contributor for leading publications, including *The Times* and *Financial Times* newspapers and *The Spectator*, *Apollo* and *Frieze* magazines, among others.

IRINA JOHNSTONE is a lyricist, dramatist, artist and gallerist. Her writings include poetic works which formed the lyrics for three critically acclaimed albums by the British group Thirsty: *Thirsty*, released in 2014; *Albatross*, released in 2016; and *Nomad*, released in 2018. Her dramatic work, *Oedipus.Complex*, is being adapted for a musical play. Irina is the owner of Three Highgate, an art gallery and creative hub in Highgate, where she is currently curating a programme of art exhibitions and writing and poetry events.